MINERALS

By Chris and Helen Pellant

Gareth Stevens
Publishing

Please visit our web site at **www.garethstevens.com**. For a free catalog describing Gareth Stevens Publishing's list of high-quality books, call 1-800-542-2595 (USA) or 1-800-387-3178 (Canada). Gareth Stevens Publishing's fax: 1-877-542-2596

Library of Congress Cataloging-in-Publication Data

Pellant, Chris.
    Minerals / Chris and Helen Pellant. — U.S. ed.
       p. cm. — (Rock stars)
    Includes index.
    ISBN-10: 0-8368-9224-0   ISBN-13: 978-0-8368-9224-6 (lib. bdg.)
    1. Minerals—Juvenile literature. I. Pellant, Helen. II. Title.
  QE365.2.P445 2009
  549—dc22   2008016121

This North American edition first published in 2009 by
Gareth Stevens Publishing
A Weekly Reader® Company
1 Reader's Digest Road
Pleasantville, NY 10570-7000 USA

This U.S. edition copyright © 2009 by Gareth Stevens, Inc. Original edition copyright © 2008 by ticktock Media Ltd. First published in Great Britain in 2008 by ticktock Media Ltd., 2 Orchard Business Centre, North Farm Road, Tunbridge Wells, Kent, TN2 3XF.

ticktock Project Editor: Julia Adams   ticktock Project Designer: Emma Randall

For Gareth Stevens:
Senior Managing Editor: Lisa M. Herrington   Creative Director: Lisa Donovan
Senior Editor: Barbara Bakowski   Electronic Production Manager: Paul Bodley

Picture credits (t = top; b = bottom; c = center; l = left; r = right):
age fotostock/Superstock: 20tr. Jon Arnold Images Ltd./Alamy: 7. E.R. Degginger/Science Photo Library: 22ft. ephotocorp/Alamy: 11b. Patrice Fury/Rex Features: 22t. GC Minerals/Alamy: 23cl. Jennie Hart/Alamy: 15br. Herris.fr/SuperStock: 5t. David Martyn Hughes/Alamy: 3l, 21br. iStock: 4l, 5br, 10bcA, 14cr, 15bl, 15cr, 23tr, 23bl. David Lees/Corbis: 10bcC. Chris and Helen Pellant: 7tr, 10blC, 13tr, 13br, 14bl, 15tr, 16tl, 16cl, 16tr, 16cr, 16br, 17tl, 17bl, 18br, 19cr, 19br, 20cl, 20ccr, 20bl, 20br, 21tl, 21bl, 21tr, 23br, 24tl. Scientifica/Visuals Unlimited/Alamy: 12l. Shutterstock: 1, 2, 3 A, B, C, D, E, F, G, H, J, K, 4tl, 4c, 4r, 5bl, 5bc, 6tl, 6b, 8tl, 8cl, 8–9, 9t, 9b, 10tl, 10cr, 12tl, 12cr, 12bl, 12br, 14tl, 14bc, 14br x2, 15tl, 15cl, 15bl, 15br, 16bl, 17cl, 17tr, 17cr, 17br, 18tr, 18cr, 18bl, 19tl, 19tr, 19cl, 19bl, 20tl, 21cl, 21cr, 22b, 23tl, 23cr. Andrew Syred/Science Photo Library: 8bl. *The Artist's Parents*, 1813 (panel), Wilkie, Sir David (1785-1841)/© National Gallery of Scotland, Edinburgh, Scotland/The Bridgeman Art Library: 10bcB. Javier Trueba/Science Photo Library: 22c. Visual Arts Library (London)/ Alamy: 11t. Charles D. Winters: 10blB.

Every effort has been made to trace copyright holders, and we apologize in advance for any omissions. We would be pleased to insert the appropriate acknowledgments in any subsequent edition of this publication.

Printed in the United States of America

3 4 5 6 7 8 9 10 09

Contents

Mineral Collector

Words that appear in **bold** are explained in the glossary.

What Are Minerals?

Minerals are substances that occur naturally in the ground. There are many different types of minerals. They come in a variety of shapes and colors.

Minerals are the materials that make up rocks. Some rocks are made up of only one mineral. Other rocks contain many different minerals.

Some minerals are soft and powdery.

Some minerals are hard and shiny.

Minerals can form many different kinds of rocks.

It's a Fact!
There are more than 3,900 different minerals on Earth!

Desert rose gypsum

Minerals are important to plants, animals, and even people. For example, we need calcium to build strong bones and teeth.

People use minerals to make things, too. There are minerals in everyday products such as toothpaste, paint, and plastic.

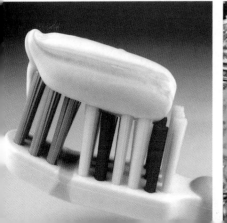

How Do Minerals Form?

Minerals can form in many different places. Most minerals form deep underground. Others form on Earth's surface.

Mineral Ingredients

Minerals, like all matter, are made up of tiny particles called **atoms**. Millions of atoms are arranged to form a solid shape.

Some minerals are made up of only one kind of atom. Other minerals are combinations of many different kinds of atoms.

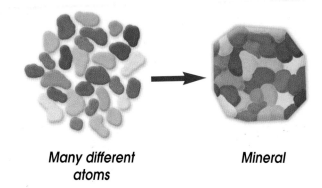

Many different atoms

Mineral

Where Minerals Form

Most minerals form far beneath Earth's surface. Deep underground, Earth is very hot and there is a lot of pressure. Sometimes hot **molten rock** bursts through a **volcano**. A volcano is a hole in Earth's crust, or outer layer. Molten rock on Earth's surface is called **lava**. When lava cools, the chemicals in it form minerals.

Molten rock sometimes bursts to Earth's surface.

From Mineral to Rock

Rocks can form when minerals join together. Rocks that form from hot molten rock are called **igneous rocks**.

Sometimes the heat and pressure under Earth's surface changes minerals. They form new rocks, called **metamorphic rocks**.

Diorite is an igneous rock. It is made up of feldspar and hornblende.

Some minerals form on Earth's surface when water **evaporates**. This is the Dead Sea, in southwestern Asia. When the water evaporates, salt is left! The Dead Sea is the saltiest body of water in the world.

Mineral Shapes

One way to identify a mineral is to look at its shape. Most minerals form naturally as **crystals**. Each mineral has its own crystal shape. Crystals have smooth, flat **faces** and straight edges.

Quartz has crystals that form in long six-sided columns.

<< A crystal is a group of atoms arranged in a pattern to form a regular shape. Some crystals are **symmetric**. Their shape looks the same from all sides.

<< This picture was taken through a microscope. It shows the crystals of table salt. Salt is made up of **cube**-shaped crystals.

Roses, Bubbles, and Other Shapes

This type of gypsum is called >> desert rose. It looks like the petals of a rose flower! This mineral forms in deserts around the world.

<< Copper sometimes forms in a shape that looks like a plant. It is called a **dendritic**, or tree-like, shape.

This dark red-brown >> mineral is hematite. It often forms in rounded bubble shapes.

Mineral Colors

Minerals can be many different colors. A mineral's color can help you identify it. Colorful minerals have been used in many different ways for thousands of years.

Mineral Paintings

Long ago, people used crushed minerals in paint. They mixed the minerals with animal fat to make a paste.

  In 1500 B.C., Egyptians used the mineral realgar to create bright orange paint.

  In the Middle Ages (about A.D. 500 to 1450), cinnabar was used to make bright red paint.

 In 16th-century Europe, artists used orpiment in paintings. Its name comes from Latin and means "golden paint."

Today, we know that these minerals are poisonous. People no longer use them to make paint.

Mineral Makeup

People in many cultures have used minerals as makeup. Women in ancient Rome whitened their skin with powder that was made of **arsenic**. They did not know it was poisonous!

Mineral Dye

For thousands of years, minerals such as lazurite have been used to make dyes. People in many ancient cultures used powdered minerals to color their clothes.

It's a Fact!
The earliest humans used minerals in their cave paintings.

In ancient India, clothing was brilliantly colored. Many of the dyes were made from minerals.

How Hard Are Minerals?

We use a scale with 10 points to measure the hardness of a mineral. You can use everyday objects to test minerals.

If you can scratch a mineral with a penknife, you know the mineral is softer than 5½. If you can scratch a mineral with a fingernail, you know it is softer than 2½.

It is easy to scratch some minerals. Others are hard to scratch. Testing the hardness of a mineral can help you identify it.

Penknife blade: 5½

Caution: Always ask an adult to help you use a penknife. The blade is very sharp!

Coin: 3½

Fingernail: 2½

Diamond: 10

Corundum: 9

Beryl: 8

Quartz: 7

Feldspar: 6

Apatite: 5

Fluorite: 4

Calcite: 3

Gypsum: 2

Talc: 1

10	
9	
8	
7	
6	
5	
4	
3	
2	
1	

Diamonds were found in South Africa in the 1800s. There are many diamond **mines** in that country. Diamond is the hardest mineral.

It's a Fact!
You can use minerals to test the hardness of other minerals! Harder minerals will scratch softer ones.

Talc is the softest mineral. You can scratch it with a fingernail. It is ground up to make baby powder.

How We Use Minerals

Minerals provide us with an amazing variety of useful materials. Important metals such as iron and copper come from minerals.

Minerals in Jewelry

People use minerals to make beautiful jewelry. Silver and gold are rare minerals. Rubies, sapphires, and diamonds are minerals called **gemstones**. They are cut and polished for use in jewelry.

Hematite

This bubble-shaped mineral supplies most of the world's iron. Iron is heated and made into steel. People use iron and steel to make thousands of things, from bridges to cooking pots!

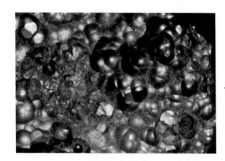

Hematite

Steel

Bridge

Cooking pot

Chalcopyrite

This mineral is mined and made into the soft metal copper. For thousands of years, people have used copper to produce many everyday items.

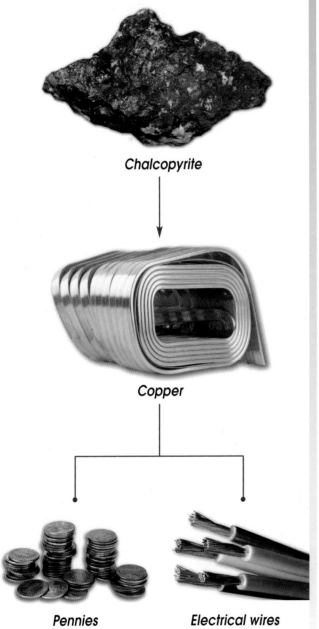

Chalcopyrite

Copper

Pennies

Electrical wires

Gypsum

This soft mineral is dried and ground into powder. The powder is used to make plaster for walls and ceilings—and even for casts to protect broken bones!

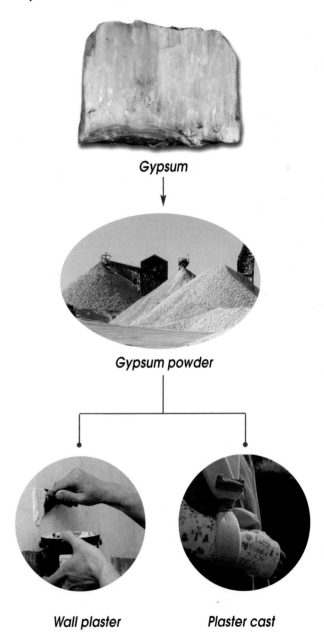

Gypsum

Gypsum powder

Wall plaster

Plaster cast

Mineral Collector

Actinolite

COLOR: green
FOUND: in metamorphic rocks
HARDNESS: 5–6

Augite

COLOR: black or dark green
FOUND: in igneous rocks
HARDNESS: 6

Garnet

COLOR: red, green, yellow, or black
FOUND: in metamorphic rocks
HARDNESS: 6½–7½

Hornblende

COLOR: black or dark green
FOUND: in igneous rocks
HARDNESS: 6

Mica

COLOR: silvery white, yellow, green, purple, brown, or black
FOUND: in igneous and metamorphic rocks
HARDNESS: 2½

Olivine

COLOR: green
FOUND: in igneous rocks
HARDNESS: 7

Feldspar

COLOR: white, pink, or gray
FOUND: in igneous and metamorphic rocks
HARDNESS: 6

Kyanite

COLOR: blue, green, yellow, or black
FOUND: in metamorphic rocks
HARDNESS: 5½–7

Quartz

COLOR: white, pink, purple, yellow, brown, green, black, or clear
FOUND: in most rocks and in **mineral veins**
HARDNESS: 7

Getting Started

To become a mineral collector, you need to have a kit of tools.

- a strong backpack for the minerals you find

- cloth or plastic bags to protect the minerals you collect

- a rock hammer for breaking up loose rocks

- goggles to wear when hammering. Rock splinters may get in your eyes.

- a magnifying glass to see close-up details

- a notebook and a pen for writing details about the minerals you've collected

Mineral Collector

Arsenopyrite

COLOR: silver
FOUND: in mineral veins
HARDNESS: 6

Barite

COLOR: white, yellow, gray, or clear
FOUND: in mineral veins
HARDNESS: 3½

Cassiterite

COLOR: brown or black
FOUND: in mineral veins
HARDNESS: 6–7

Chalcopyrite

COLOR: brassy yellow
FOUND: in mineral veins
HARDNESS: 4

Galena

COLOR: gray
FOUND: in mineral veins
HARDNESS: 2½

Siderite

COLOR: brown or yellow
FOUND: in mineral veins
HARDNESS: 4

Calcite

COLOR: white, gray, brown, or clear
FOUND: in mineral veins or limestone
HARDNESS: 3

Fluorite

COLOR: blue, purple, green, yellow, or white
FOUND: in mineral veins
HARDNESS: 4

Sphalerite

COLOR: black or brown
FOUND: in mineral veins
HARDNESS: 4

Finding Minerals

Mining is the removal of minerals from the earth. When people dig mines, they take out material and put it on a huge pile called a mine heap.

> **CAUTION:**
> Do not go to a mine without an adult present. Never enter an active mine.

You can find minerals in other places, too:

- Mineral veins in rocks or hillsides may be full of quartz or other minerals.

Mineral vein

- Colorful pebbles at the beach are made up of one or more minerals.

Mineral Collector

Agate

COLOR: pink, red, or blue
FOUND: in cavities in lava
HARDNESS: 7

Chrysocolla

COLOR: green or blue
FOUND: in copper deposits
HARDNESS: 4

Gypsum

COLOR: white, yellow, brown, or green
FOUND: in dried-out deposits
HARDNESS: 2

Pyrite

COLOR: pale golden yellow
FOUND: in mineral veins and in many rocks, especially slate
HARDNESS: 6½

Topaz

COLOR: gray, yellow, green, brown, orange, or purple
FOUND: in granite
HARDNESS: 8

Tourmaline

COLOR: green, pink, yellow, brown, or black
FOUND: in granite and metamorphic rocks
HARDNESS: 7

Dioptase

COLOR: dark green
FOUND: in copper-rich mineral veins
HARDNESS: 5

Rhodochrosite

COLOR: pink or red
FOUND: in mineral veins
HARDNESS: 4

Vanadinite

COLOR: red or orange
FOUND: in lead-rich mineral veins
HARDNESS: 3

Making Displays

When you have gathered some mineral samples, you may want to display them.

Here are a few tips on how best to display your collection.

- Clean minerals carefully with a soft paintbrush.

- Make card trays for your samples.

- Make labels for each tray section. Write the name of the mineral and where you found it.

- Keep your display in a glass-fronted cabinet or on a shelf. Wrap and store other minerals in drawers.

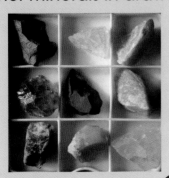

Record Breakers

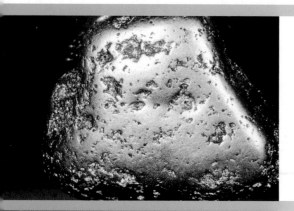

Most Precious Metal

Platinum is much more valuable than gold because platinum is so rare. It is used to make jewelry, watches, coins, chemical containers, and even car parts!

Some large diamonds cut from Cullinan

Largest Diamond

The Cullinan diamond was the biggest diamond ever found. It was discovered in 1905 in South Africa. The stone was cut into nine large and 96 small diamonds.

Biggest Crystals

The Cave of Crystals in Chihuahua, Mexico, has the largest natural crystals in the world. The gypsum crystals are 36 feet (11 meters) long. They formed over millions of years.

Most Common Mineral on Earth's Surface

Naturally formed ice is a mineral, even though water isn't. Ice is the most common mineral on Earth's surface. It covers at least one-tenth of our planet.

Did You Know?

The ancient Egyptians were some of the earliest people to use gold to make jewelry.

Diamonds are so hard, they cannot be scratched by any other material. Diamond is 40 times harder than talc!

Quartz crystals are used in some watches and clocks to keep time.

Pyrite, or "fool's gold," is a common mineral that people often mistake for real gold.

Gold is a very soft mineral. You can scratch it with a coin!

There are 16 main types of quartz, in colors from yellow and pink to purple and black!

The mineral realgar forms in bright red crystals. People used it to color fireworks until they discovered it was poisonous.

Minerals don't exist only in rocks. Our bones and teeth are made of minerals, too.

Sometimes minerals form in rock cracks. These shapes are called mineral veins.

Glossary

arsenic a gray metal-like material that is poisonous

atoms tiny particles that make up all matter

crystals solid forms with atoms arranged in a pattern to form a regular shape

cube a solid shape with six square sides

dendritic branching like a tree

evaporates turns from a liquid into a gas

faces naturally formed flat surfaces of a crystal

gemstones minerals that can be cut and polished for use in jewelry

igneous rocks rocks formed by the hardening of molten material from deep within Earth

lava molten rock on Earth's surface that usually comes out of a volcano

metamorphic rocks rocks formed when heat or pressure, or both, cause changes in rock minerals

minerals naturally formed materials that make up rocks

mineral veins thin masses of minerals that run through rock layers

mines pits in the earth from which minerals are removed

molten rock rock that it is extremely hot and that flows like a liquid

platinum a shiny, silvery metal used in jewelry, electronics, and coins

symmetric balanced on either side of a dividing line or around a center

volcano a hole in Earth's crust through which molten rock bursts to the surface

Index